Things That Matter: Returning Heaven to Creation

By Bob Mumford

LIFECHANGERS®

P.O. Box 3709 ❖ Cookeville, TN 38502
931.520.3730 ❖ lc@lifechangers.org

Bob Sutton was instrumental in helping me put together the pieces of this Plumbline. Bob nurtures the body of Christ as a pastor and educator. He served many years as an editor of *New Wine* magazine. I would like to express my gratitude for his friendship and his assistance in making *Things That Matter* a reality.

Unless otherwise noted, all Scripture quotations are taken from *The New American Standard Bible*, The Lockman Foundation, 1960, 1962, 1963, 1968, 1972, 1973, 1975, 1977. All rights reserved.

PLUMBLINE

Published by:

LIFECHANGERS ®
L I B R A R Y S E R I E S

P.O. Box 3709 | Cookeville, TN 38502
(800) 521-5676 | www.lifechangers.org

Things That Matter:
Returning Heaven to Creation

By Bob Mumford

Intro: My personal integrity seems to require giving witness to an increased sense of spiritual conflict as I wrote this Plumbline. Would you, as you read, be aware of the spiritual reality that emerges within the concepts themselves? I am confident that which is between the lines will allow us to enter the Kingdom, which promises greater intimacy with God the Father.

Early Saturday morning, July 24, 2021, Judith and I were having coffee on the porch. We were in a very good place. The morning was glorious; purpose seemed to be exuding from the sunlight and the trees. Without warning I began to experience a sudden and rather severe physical reaction. We later understood this to be the onset of Covid symptoms. Fever, mental confusion, and the sense of despair were totally overwhelming. Judith and I both tested positive for Covid. Everything physical, mental, emotional, and spiritual became progressively bleak. Every choice and action became increasingly difficult and wrapped in darkness.

In my 90+ years I have never experienced such physical distress. For several weeks we quite literally walked through "the valley of the shadow of death." Often, I feared for Judith's life. We are most grateful to our daughter, Beth, who was ever present at risk to herself.

Intense suffering has a way of clarifying the things that really matter. Only four things were important: Judith's recovery; not wanting to leave Judith alone; some relief from the relentless, overwhelming pain and fatigue; and fully completing the purpose for which Christ called me.

Jesus has a way of clarifying what really matters. He said it something like this, *"What matters first is finding the government of God and then aligning yourself with His purpose. Then everything else will fall into place."*[1]

During this deep crisis of life, the Lord said very clearly, "You must see yourself as a stable." I understood He was referring to the stable in which Jesus was born. I'm human with all kinds of human complexities, insecurities, and short comings. When I saw myself as a stable, I understood something of God's purpose and plan for my life. My spiritual quest with the Lord over the last 70 years could be summarized as a journey that starts with being born in a stable and ends with rest in the New Jerusalem.

God the Father chose Jesus, the incarnate Son, to be born in a stable. His purpose was more than our singing "Away in a Manger" and feeling warm and fuzzy once a year. The Creator of the Universe chose to enter this world as a human; to live as a man; to experience this world with all its pain,

---

1 Matthew 6:33, Mumford paraphrase

grief, and difficulties to become the last Adam and the second man. He walked through this life without undue privilege, rank, or resources to demonstrate what it is like to live as God intended at creation. He so identified with humanity that He most often referred to Himself as the Son of Man. If we are able see ourselves as a stable, then we can begin to have Christ being born in us.

I came to know the Lord at age twelve. But because of severe, unexpected persecution, I rather forcefully and angrily demanded that the Lord get out of my life. As most of you know, I walked away from His Person for twelve years. Dramatically, He took hold of me at the end of those twelve years, imparting to me an absolute passion to lay hold of Him. Immediately, without full knowledge, I set myself on a journey following in the steps of Abraham who was looking for a city with permanent foundations whose builder and maker is God—the New Jerusalem.[2]

As an aside, let's put Abraham's story in perspective. Abraham and his father, Terah, had worshipped the gods of Babylon (Chaldeans) in the city of Ur.[3] The Babylonian pantheon consisted of hundreds of national and local gods each governing a particular function of life or a given territory, each demanding certain loyalties and offerings or sacrifices. Make no mistake, these were real spiritual

---

2 Please see Hebrews 11:10; 12:22; 13:14
3 Joshua 24:2-3

entities operating under the serpent's authority, bringing corruption, darkness, and bondage to humanity. In the midst of this darkness and oppression, the glory of God appeared to Abraham.[4]

Babylon is one of the important sub-themes of the Bible's portrayal of human history. Abraham, the father of faith and the blesser of the earth, is called out of Babylon. In Revelation, Babylon is seen as the great opposing force to the Kingdom of Christ and is defeated forever.

Having seen the glory of the Most High God, Abraham journeyed to Canaan leaving the spiritual confusion of Ur. In this new land he would look for a spiritual, heavenly city "which has foundations, who's architect and builder is God."[5] Abraham was a wealthy man. Had he chosen, he could have founded a city that was more permanent and secure than the life of a nomad. Abraham lived in tents because he understood he was on a journey as an alien in a land that was still ruled by the gods of Babylon. If he had built a city it would have been of his own efforts and as such would have invited the local gods to take possession. Canaan became Abraham's "stable"—the place where God brought Abraham to spiritual maturity.

Whether or not we fully understand it, each of us is on a similar journey. We have been called out of the confusion of the gods of Babylon. We

4 Acts 7:2
5 Hebrews 11:10

are looking for the New Jerusalem. It is urgent we understand the essence of our journey from the foundation of God's revealed truth. We will not bother to rehash all that we already believe; rather, we will challenge ourselves to consider that what we have been taught is in the process of expansion. What we hold as biblical truth is most likely not wrong but inadequate. God wants to align us with the actual journey that He, as our Father, has in mind!

This is critical because what we believe about the purposes of God governs how we see and respond to the future. Our world is changing with increasing rapidity. If we don't understand Father's plan and purpose, it is possible we could miss it. Recall that the Jews of Jesus' day had a detailed grasp of the Scriptures yet tragically missed the purpose that God had for them. It simply does not make sense that Israel could totally miss the Messiah!

Our desire is to focus on the "end game" where Father has focused His goal for human history. Most of us would agree that the consummation of redemptive history is the Kingdom of God being established on the earth. Kingdom is an archaic word; it carries many connotations that a twenty-first century, post-modern person may not grasp. When defined Biblically, Kingdom signifies *God's irrevocable and invisible presence that gives direction and purpose to the entire earth and all humanity* whether we are fully aware of it or not.

Kingdom keeps on coming whether we believe it or not!

Please hear me: His Kingdom is not a place, an institution, a prescribed life-style, or a set of doctrinal beliefs. *His Kingdom is a person.* God is Spirit. Entering His Kingdom is a relational encounter with God's person, a "Sweet Society" of Father, Son, and Holy Spirit. This is stated in Mt. 28:19, which describes our being welcomed into that Sweet Society by means of water baptism. Baptism expresses our intentionality to embrace Christ in death and resurrection. Water baptism is not primarily about forgiveness—it is primarily governmental. Our eager embrace of death and resurrection says to Father God that we desire to know Him and His purpose in the earth. We are seeking the city for which Abraham was looking!

To be exceedingly clear, very little is guaranteed and nothing is automatic. Jesus' final instructions before He went to sit at Father's right hand were: You don't need to know about all the Father has planned. You will be empowered to tell the hurting world there is a new government on the earth. Show them how to live under that government, baptize them into it, and teach them what I taught you, and I'll be with you until you finish the job.[6]

There is *human responsibility* in God's plan and purpose for the times in which we are living. It is not merely surviving until the end. What is the long

---

6 My paraphrase of Acts 1:7-8 and Matthew 28:18-20.

view of what God intends? What really matters on our journey from the stable to the New Jerusalem?

I would like to present for your consideration six realities that I believe matter most urgently if we are to engage and satisfy all that the Father has called us to be and do. These are "realities" because they are more than concepts or principles. They are modes of living and being that were modeled by Christ in His incarnation. I will identify these six, in brief, then expand each in a manner that will allow us to embrace and engage them with greater clarity and integrity. They are:

1. Discover and embrace the purpose God had in mind for you when He personally engaged you.
2. Begin to intentionally reside and abide in the "living room".
3. Embrace Agape as the only feasible absolute. Agape is God's governing force.
4. Yoke yourself with Christ in authentic altruism.
5. Hold family as the foundational rock of society on earth.
6. Join Christ, as a participant, in giving the world its Father back.

Discover and embrace God's revealed purpose

This diagram is inadequate and essentially misrepresents God's intended biblical purpose:

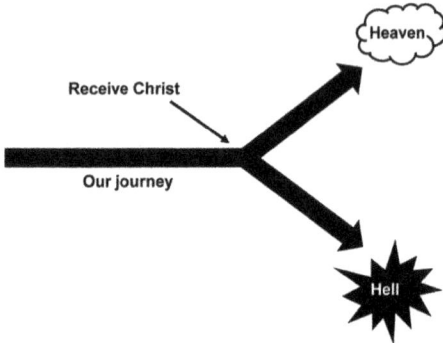

This theory implies that the only thing that matters is whether we are headed for Heaven or Hell. Does it matter where we end up? Of course. However, we have unintentionally lost biblical purpose and destiny: the very content of the message of Jesus. What really matters is our contribution and participation as co-heirs with Christ in seeking the restoration of God's Fatherhood to the hurting earth.

Stephen Covey, the author of *Seven Habits of Highly Effective People*, coined the phrase: "The main thing is to keep the main thing the main thing." All too often we do not fully grasp what the main thing is from God's point of view. We are familiar with the expression, "you can't see the forest for the trees." We have become so focused on what is immediately in front of us that we fail to comprehend the big picture of what surrounds us. God calls us to live in His epic meta-narrative in which we are being called to participate. Until we fully comprehend the magnitude of "the forest" of His purpose, we will not be able to appreciate and embrace our own individual place as one of His "trees of righteousness."

Without becoming overly technical, it is helpful to understand that there are two Greek words in the New Testament that are often translated "will" (e.g., this is the will of God). One word, *thelema,* means, "a wish" or "a desire." The second word, *boulema,* means, "purpose," "counsel," or, in theological terms, "the immutable counsel."

When the New Testament speaks of the will of God, it is often referring to that which God desires or wishes, *thelema.* For example, Matthew 6:10, "Your will (desire / wishes) be done on earth as it is in heaven." The nature of the Father is most often not one of demanding but of expressing His desires and intentions. He is looking for a free response of human respect and love. *Boulema,* on the other hand, expresses the determined purpose of God, which He will ultimately bring to fruition regardless of human corruption or the resistance of the power of darkness.

Once God declares His purpose, it is

unchangeable[7]. Speaking of God's sovereign purpose, Paul writes in Romans 9:19, "Who resists His will [*boulema*]?" Paul spoke to the elders at Ephesus, "I did not shrink from declaring to you the whole purpose [*boulema*] of God." Paul's desire was for them to understand that God has an immutable counsel in order that they might align themselves with it and order their lives and intentions in accordance. From prison Paul would later write to them that they had been "predestined according to His purpose who works all things after the counsel [*boulema*] of His will [*thelema*]."[8]

Ultimately, if we fail to align ourselves with God's purposes for our lives, we may discover ourselves living without purpose. Wealth, fame, or success make no difference in preventing the choice to take one's own life, either suddenly or incrementally. Choosing alcohol, drugs, sex, more and brighter gadgets, longer vacations to more exotic places, or any of a smorgasbord of options to breathe some meaning into the loss of purpose will consume us at the core of our beings.

Please pause and thoughtfully ponder these questions: How did I come to be where I am today? How did the Lord alter my life's course, imparting His call in my heart? It is called *the invisible government of God.* Some embrace His call as very little children. Others hear His call throughout their

7 See Hebrews 6:17
8 Ephesians 1:11

lives. Some resisted, fought, and wrestled but are here now. When I told God to get out of my life at twelve years old, I think He probably chuckled a little. He knew His purpose for me, and He let me go my own way until the day He had set to lay hold of me. Each of us are called to be participants in the sweeping meta-narrative of God's relationship with His creation and with humankind.

A Good Beginning

It has become increasingly clear that most people's Bibles start in Genesis chapter three—at the fall. We usually start with sin consciousness, human failure, separation, death, thorns, and thistles. But the Lord didn't start His story there. God said, "It's good!" He speaks "good" seven times in Genesis 1 and 2. After He created humankind, He looked at everything and said, "It is *very* good!"

Everything was "very good" because God is good. Everything He does and creates is good. In a very limited sense creation is an incarnation of God's invisible attributes, eternal power, and divine nature. I have come to see this as the "first incarnation," God manifesting Himself in the time/space Universe.

What should that say to us about God, His creation, His purposes, and His ultimate intentions? When Jesus walked the earth He *"went about doing good,"* healing, delivering, and setting people free.[9]

9 See Acts 10:38

When Jesus approached hurting people, He didn't tell them how sinful they were nor about going to Heaven. He brought the Kingdom of Heaven to them! He restored them to what was good. By the presence of His person, He introduces us to Father's family. This family is filled with His life of restoration, healing, purpose, and freedom. He wants us to live in what is good, as we were created, eating from the Tree of Life.

Creation faith goes back before the fall where Father's wishes, will, and purpose were done on the earth. God gave His original pair the responsibility of ruling creation on His behalf. It looks something like this:

In God's mind, Heaven and earth are one. God's purposes on the earth were manifested and administrated through Adam and Eve. The garden was intended as the place of God's presence. It is the place from which creation's couple would have extended order and beauty through their offspring to the entire planet.

Choosing disobedience allowed separation between Heaven and Earth. Through the process of increased corruption the original couple became increasingly separated.

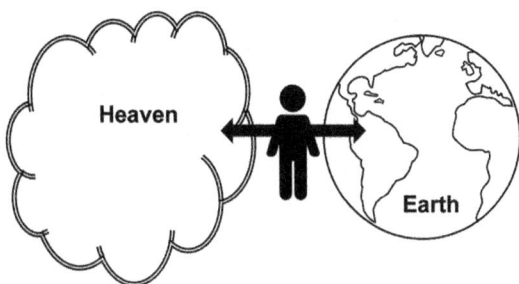

That sinful transgression initiated a man-made separation. God could have discarded Adam and Eve, made a new pair, recommissioned them, and started afresh. However, the fact that God did not set Adam and Eve aside reveals something most profound about His nature. God has chosen to *share His sovereignty* with humanity as part of His imparted image. Man made the separation, and a man would have to take the responsibility to restore what had been lost. Tragically, humanity would become increasingly incapable of doing so. The race lost the Life of the divine image and became hobbled by the ever-accelerating force of corruption. "In the day you eat of it, dying you will die."[10]

Yet, no matter how far humanity departs from the knowledge and presence of God, the memory of God as a Father in that garden, heaven on earth, is deeply imprinted in the human psyche. We earnestly strive to make our own heaven on Earth, rebuilding our own Eden. We call it the worker's paradise, the American dream, the great society, even the "kingdom of God." They are envisioned and built out of the corrupted human souls rather than the Life of God, our humanly created "Edens" must ultimately wither, corrupt, and fail.

God, as a Father, refused to rush to man's rescue. To do so would have overreached the sovereignty God had given to all humanity. Because a man had abused his authority, only a man, could bring heaven back to earth. God chose to invade earth with the second man who came from Heaven[11], the Last Adam, incarnating Himself in the pattern son.

Jesus is the *second incarnation.* The Father manifested Himself in human flesh. He gave the Son authority to put down the rebellion, to begin the work of reconciliation, and to release the power of His resurrection into the earth to begin reversing the corruption of death. It looks like this:

---

10 Genesis 2:17 Literal Hebrew
11 1 Corinthians 15:47

Incarnation!

The kingdom did *not* come *in* Christ. The Father *gave* the Kingdom to Jesus, and Jesus was totally faithful. He was born in a stable, grew in favor with God and man, matured as a human, learned obedience, and always did the things His father wished. As He approached His passion and death He told His disciples:

> You are those who have stood by Me in My trials; and just as My Father has granted Me a kingdom, I grant you that you may eat and drink at My table in My kingdom. . . [12]

Jesus had completed the work His Father had given Him. He was able to declare, "My Father has granted Me a kingdom." The Kingdom was given to Christ by the Father, and He had been faithful over all that the Father had given Him.[13]

---

12 Luke 22:28-30
13 See Hebrews 3:1-6

Although He was a Son, He <u>learned obedience</u> from the things which He suffered. And having been made perfect, [From the Greek teleios, better translated "mature" or "complete"] He became to all those who obey Him the source of eternal salvation.[14]

Full participation in the Kingdom of God cannot be automatically granted to every believer. That may shock some people's doctrine, but if we carefully examine the New Testament, we discover that the Kingdom of God can be inherited, entered into, and taken away. Why is this important? Jesus would next say to His disciples, "I grant you to have a part in my kingdom." Why were the disciples granted participation in the Kingdom? Jesus had said to them, "You have stood by Me in My trials." They had been faithful; humanly responsible.

It is most sobering to realize that it is possible to call Jesus "Lord", minister in the supernatural, but continue to do things our own way failing to realize authentic entrance into the Kingdom of God[15]. Loss of Kingdom as our inheritance has nothing to do with Christ's redemptive gift. Kingdom resides within the sphere of becoming reconciled with God as our Father. The disciples had encountered the Life of the Kingdom in Jesus, and when others left, they stayed with Him.

14 Hebrews 5:8-9
15 See Matthew 7:21- 23

Jesus invaded earth as God's governing purpose almost without recognition. He came in a stable, and throughout His life began to lay the foundations of the city for which Abraham had been searching. Abraham was seeking the governing purpose of God, the invisible New Jerusalem. God had ordained that His government on the earth would be established in, and flow out of, Jerusalem and especially Zion, the place of His Presence[16].

God gave the Kingdom to Israel, but they failed and/or refused to produce the fruit of that Kingdom. Therefore, Jesus declared to the Jewish leaders of His day that "the Kingdom of God will be taken away from you and given to a people [nation], producing the fruit of it."[17] After His resurrection, Jesus told His disciples, "All authority has been given to Me in heaven and on earth [Father had given Him the Kingdom]. Go therefore and make disciples of all the nations. . . .." Jesus gave His Kingdom to the apostles, and through them He began to establish a new nation, a new race, one new man, the New Jerusalem. A new governing authority was incarnated and released on the earth.

The opposition to a new government, new covenant, and new forms of righteousness on the earth was fierce. The disinherited gods of Babylon, reincarnated in religious and political institutions, were not about to allow a new Adam to establish a

---

16 Isaiah 2:2-4; Micah 4:1-3
17 Matthew 21:43

foothold within their empires. Because the rulers of that age were held captive by darkness, they could not comprehend the wisdom of God and crucified the Lord of glory. They did not understand that crucifixion would result in resurrection. The resurrection released the power of God and the Holy Spirit over the earth activating the Kingdom invasion.

By His crucifixion and resurrection Christ broke the dominion of the ruling empires and brought to nothing the power of death. The work of the cross was to bring Heaven and Earth back together again. "He made peace through the blood of His cross."

Through the resurrection, the Spirit of Christ has been made available incarnationally to the assembly of God's people. The kingdom reality is being birthed in my person and in each of you reading this. Heaven is invading through us in a new birth, a new man, a new creation, new heaven, a new earth, and a

New Jerusalem. We are God's love bringing healing to a hurting world. We are called and predestined to be the *third incarnation* of God's presence and person in earth.

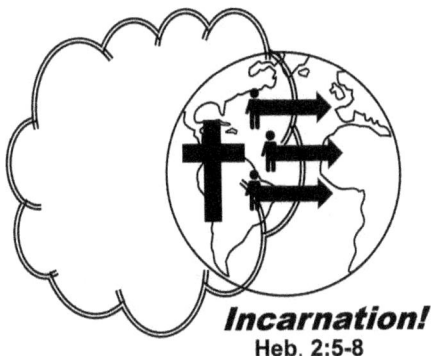

Incarnation!
Heb. 2:5-8

It is clear from the New Testament that we have been given the authority and the power to carry the message and mission of Jesus into all the world. Father is working to conform us to the image of His Son in order that we might manifest His person in the same manner that Jesus did. As the writer of Hebrews declares:

> For He did not subject to angels the world to come, concerning which we are speaking. But one has testified somewhere, saying, "What is man, that you remember him? Or the son of man, that you are concerned about him? You have made him for a little while lower than the angels; You have crowned him

with glory and honor, and have appointed him over the works of your hands; You have put all things in subjection under his feet." For in subjecting all things to him, He left nothing that is not subject to him. But now we do not yet see all things subjected to him.[18]

When Christ encountered me, I had nothing to offer Him but a stable. When He laid hold of me it was a face-to-face encounter with the governing intention of God. It was not particularly a church encounter, an intellectual encounter, nor an emotional encounter. When we are laid hold of by the risen Christ, we immediately begin to seek "that city" which Abraham sought, the invisible governing force of God, Himself. Christ challenged me with a "Kingdom offer". Heaven and forgiveness were not an issue at that point. The city of God's making is not a place where we're going or an institution we can join. His Kingdom is a Person who has taken up residence within us. He is the spiritual reality that captures our very person. Here is Paul's testimony:

I press on so that I may lay hold of that for which also I was laid hold of by Christ Jesus. Brethren, I do not regard myself as having laid hold of it yet; but one thing I do: forgetting what lies behind and reaching forward to what lies

18 Hebrews 2:5-8

ahead, I press on toward the goal for the prize of the upward <u>call of God in Christ Jesus</u>[19] [Underlines mine].

Like Paul, I wanted to know the "that". What did Christ have in His mind when He laid hold of me? When I met Christ, I knew He had a purpose for me. Something about me mattered to Him. I was not satisfied to be saved and go to heaven. What does His purpose for you look like? How are you going to engage it? Life without purpose is hardly worth living. I am almost 91 years old at this writing, and maybe I should consider settling down a little—but I can't! His purpose has been so vital, real, and eternal that I have requested another 10 years. *What must matter most to us is what matters most to Him!*

Without question we are all stables. Can you see yourself as a stable? Your stable is the ultimate reality where the purposes of Christ do an incarnational work in you. The purpose of God is formed in our stable, then proceeds out from our stables, and moves inexorably toward the New Jerusalem.

Here's one rather dramatic example of how the Kingdom invades. When I was pastoring, I went to call on one my elders and his wife. Preparing to knock on the door I heard them verbally fighting. Being a good pastor, I didn't knock! I chose to listen.

---

19 Philippians 3:12-14

They were mad; she was saying ugly words, and he was in a rage. Suddenly I realized this was their reality, and now it was also mine. I knocked hard on the door, suddenly the fight stopped—the religion returned. They answered the door all spiritual and religious, "Pastor, so good to see you."

I said, "I heard you fighting. What are you fighting about?" She said, "We've been married six, almost seven years, and no children."

Without much forethought, I took them both by the hands. I said, in a confident, prophetic voice that was not my own: "It is not the will of God, for you to be childless. One year from today, you will hold this child in your hand, and you will know that God, as your Father, has accomplished this for you!"

Realizing what had happened I excused myself. Aware that maybe I had gone out too far, I hurried to the car, took hold of the steering wheel, and cried out, *"God, Father God, if you ever honored a prayer, you must honor that one!"* Within the year God gave them a beautiful daughter, and years later it was my privilege to have her as a student when I was a professor of New Testament at Elim Bible College. Father's Kingdom purpose appeared.

The incarnation of Christ in us is the *goodness of the Kingdom* manifesting through us. It is intentional. It is normal. This is how the kingdom works. We need to be about the business of bringing heaven back to earth. "Signs and wonders" is repeated 15 times in the New Testament.

Learning to abide in the "Living Room"

I am beginning to recognize three levels or models of living. Please picture with me a three-story house with the general living area on the ground floor, a sparsely furnished attic, and a basement. Each of these levels will aid in illustrating the range and nature of human responses when dealing with life and all the issues life seems to bring our way.

The Living Room

The graphic below represents my human responses in the "living room." When I am in the living room my identity is healthy. I am engaged, relational, and experiencing the full range of human emotions. I don't need to hide or perform. I can act and react naturally and freely. I am unthreatened, non-competitive, and free. I live within the bounds of human experience as God created me. The limits of the living room are illustrated by the dark parallel lines. Those lines are instinctive and natural. Life is as God the Father intends.

Range of Human Responses

Living Room: *Instinctive, Natural & Relational:*

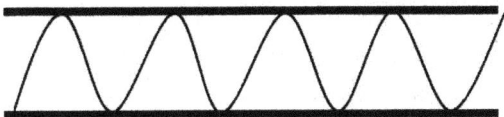

Jesus was almost always in the Living Room. He lived out the full range of human experience without embracing the temptation to do anything apart from His Father's nature and pleasure. He experienced physical pain, hunger, and fatigue. He had moments of frustration, sorrow, grief, anger, longing, and rejection. He knew joy, peace, love, friendship, exaltation, and approbation. He had to learn, resist, overcome, obey, lead, rebuke, and show tolerance and patience. He was not a placid, phlegmatic, one dimensional Dr. Spock. He lived all of His life as God designed an image-bearing person to be. *He was authentic.* He governed His person in such a way as to live freely within the bounds of human flesh without stepping outside of God's design. Because of His freedom and authenticity people were drawn to Him:

> And it happened that He was reclining at the table in his [Matthew the tax collector] house, and many tax collectors and sinners were dining with Jesus and His disciples; for there were many of them, and they were following Him. When the scribes of the Pharisees saw that He was eating with the sinners and tax collectors, they said to His disciples, "Why is He eating and drinking with tax collectors and sinners?" And hearing this, Jesus said to them, "It is not those who are healthy who need a physician,

but those who are sick; I did not come to call the righteous, but sinners."[20]

It seems unlikely that "many tax collectors and sinners" would have been attracted to a stodgy, religious lecture on how far outside the religious boundaries they were. In a similar passage in Luke, *The Message Bible* reads:

By this time a lot of men and women of doubtful reputation were hanging around Jesus, listening intently. The Pharisees and religion scholars were not pleased, not at all pleased. They growled, "He takes in sinners and eats meals with them, treating them like old friends."[21]

John told us that Life was in Jesus and that Life was the light of men. Perhaps that *Zoe*[22], the life of God in Jesus, was not some incomprehensible force. It was the substance of God's very being and *manifested goodness* in the human person of Jesus. Our image of the Father might transform somewhat if we could see Father in Jesus eating, welcoming sinners, and enjoying their company.

Sometimes we wonder how some Christians would have been comfortable hanging out with

20 Mark 2:15-17
21 Luke 15:1-2. THE MESSAGE © 2002 by Eugene H. Peterson
22 *Zoe* is the Greek word used in the New Testament for the life of God

the crowds Jesus frequented. I don't think He was eating with them so He could "win them to Jesus". He was eating with them because He enjoyed them. He genuinely wanted to be there. He wanted them to be with Him. They sat together with Jesus and His disciples, and Mark tells us that many of them were following Him. Jesus was not so concerned with getting everyone straightened out as He was demonstrating the true character of His Father.

Does being conformed to the image of the Son make you more spiritual? In one sense it does, but Father's determined issue is *to make us more human*. Christ came as the pattern son. Jesus is referred to as Son of God 58 times, but He is biblically identified as Son of Man 199 times. His self-identification was the Son of Man. One Biblical commentator expresses Son of Man as "the Human One".[23] I believe this statement most accurately captures the intent and essence of His title. Being conformed to Christ's image results in our becoming more human as God intended!

Please notice that our responses and behavior in the living room are not a flat line. There will be highs and lows. Jesus experienced the highs of real life (He rejoiced and was glad); as well as the lows (He was grieved, and He wept). He had times when He moved in great power but also in weakness. It is our natural human tendency to desire the highs

23 Howard-Brook and Anthony Gwyther, *Unveiling Empire. Reading Revelation Then and Now.* P. 140, 218, 219, 234. © 1999

and try to avoid or escape the lows. We love to experience power but are most hesitant to embrace weakness when we find ourselves in it.

Weakness was a necessary part of Jesus' humanity. First, He chose *voluntary weakness.* He chose to leave His position as Creator of the Universe and become human to the point of coming into His creation as an infant son born in a stable. Second, He experienced *circumstantial weakness* when He was tired, hungry, rejected by His own, and deserted by His friends. Finally, He endured and embraced *providential weakness* when He yielded Himself to the Father's purpose in the cross. He was crucified because of weakness, but out of His weakness on the cross, He defeated the powers of death and released the resurrection power of a New Creation upon the earth.[24]

The trail of faith through the Scriptures has been blazed by men and women who came to maturity in faith and ultimately fulfilled their God-given purpose because they walked in both circumstantial and providential weakness. Abraham and Sarah became heirs of the promise when she was barren and he was as good as dead. Paul came to Corinth in weakness and in fear and in much trembling. He "boasted" about providential weakness because out of it he would become strong in the Lord.

Passing my ninetieth year and still experiencing the after effects of COVID, I am walking in a

---

24 2 Corinthians 13:4. Also, see Acts 2:23

profundity of weakness I could never have imagined. I would now define weakness something like: things not going my way and being unable to do anything about it. However, in the midst of my weakness, I am finding a new intimacy in the Lord's presence. He is leading me into a broader and deeper experience of His Person. I am experiencing His purposes for this phase of His redemptive work in bringing the Kingdom of Heaven back to creation.

Don't be afraid to embrace weakness when it comes to your living room. It will enable us to focus more acutely on the things that really matter in life.

The Attic

In the attic, identity is distorted, overly controlled yet mismanaged, religious, ascetic, narrow, and striving. We lose or distort our humanity. Coming back to the Lord, after 12 years of going my own way, my zeal was frightening. I was determined God would see the sincerest "follower" He could imagine. I was ready to prove myself.

Range of Human Responses

Attic: *Religious, Ascetic & Self-determined*

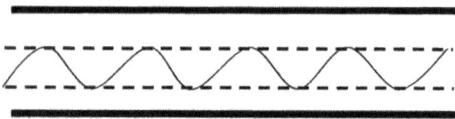

Living Room: *Instinctive, Natural & Relational*

In the attic, human experience is not governed—it is stifled! It is dominated by self-imposed or institutionally imposed, restrictions (dotted lines), which may include some or all of your beliefs and behaviors. Paul addressed the Attic in Colossians 2:16-23. Please note my emphasis in italics.

Therefore no one is to act as your judge in regard to food or drink or in respect to a festival or a new moon or a Sabbath day—things which are *a mere shadow* of what is to come; but the substance belongs to Christ. Let no one keep *defrauding you* of your prize by delighting in self-abasement and the worship of the angels, taking his stand on visions he has seen, *inflated without cause* by his fleshly mind, and *not holding fast to the head*, from whom the entire body, being supplied and held together by the joints and ligaments, grows with a growth which is from God.

If you have died with Christ to the elementary principles of the world, why, as if you were living in the world, do you submit yourself to decrees, such as, "Do not handle, do not taste, do not touch!" (Which all refer to *things destined to perish with use*)—in accordance with the commandments and teachings of men? These are matters which have, to be sure, the *appearance of wisdom* in self-made religion and self-abasement and severe treatment of the body, but are of *no value against fleshly indulgence*.

When I determined to live the holiest life humanly possible, the result was fifteen years as an ascetic, religious person keeping myself "unstained by the world." I avoided every appearance of what my religious rules declared to be "evil." I not only lived that way but let it be known to everyone else (especially my wife and three children) that this was the only way to truly "walk with the Lord." It is a miracle that Judith stayed with me and my children didn't rebel.

The person that lives in the attic is a relational loner because he or she can never let anyone else know they have normal human desires, emotions, and thoughts. The religious requirement to live in the attic is one of the reasons young people often bail out of institutional religion. By nature they are drawn to the human reality of the living room.

Attic dwellers crucified Jesus because He would not live between their dotted lines. They were threatened by the living room where life was too spontaneous, unpredictable, exposed, and real. As we read above, Jesus was inclusive, anxious to introduce everyone to the freedom of His Father's embrace. Exclusivity reigns in the attic—the world is viewed as them and us. If "they" are willing to live between our dotted lines, then "they" can become part of us.

If we retreat to the attic we enter the white-knuckle club. We make a list of "I'm gonna's": I'm gonna fast; I'm gonna confess more Bible; I'm gonna pray more; I'm never gonna say bad words again; I'm gonna be the best witness for Jesus. "Do we really mean it? Of course! What did Peter say? "Lord, even if everyone else bails on you, *I'm never gonna…"*

Jesus said, "Before tomorrow morning, you're gonna blow it." Jesus knew Peter needed to be knocked out of the attic and come down into the living room. The person in the attic is religiously hard. "Well, if you just fast and believe God, you will get out of this mess." Nothing is more injurious than the hard, religious, and demanding set of dotted lines. I've done it, and I grieve for the injuries I've caused. Please remember, we will retreat to the attic but Jesus will bring us back to the Living Room to keep us tender and real.

Probably some of the darkest spiritual forces in the Universe are in the attic. Human history's most heinous and monstrous conflicts have been centered around "them/us" categories. They evoke the passion and devotion of a religion. The master of darkness seduces us between the dotted lines of religion, political philosophy, social values, or a utopian vision deluding us into thinking we can be like the gods. Then, inflated with corrupted minds and ungoverned desires, we destroy one another.

As followers of Christ we have been called into Him for the express purpose of *incarnating the humanity of Jesus* and inviting the world to enter and experience the living room.

The Basement

In the basement, identity becomes dark, depressed, and without joy or hope. We may become manic, hedonistic, addictive, and mood-centered. (Let me be quick to say this is not someone who may be bi-polar, which is a treatable medical condition).

Range of Human Responses

Attic: *Religious, Ascetic & Self-determined*

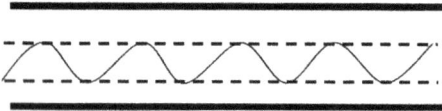

Living Room: *Instinctive, Natural & Relational*

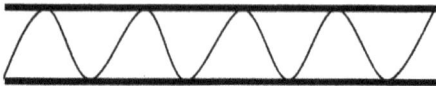

Basement: *Deviant, Broken Loose:* **Manic / Hedonistic**

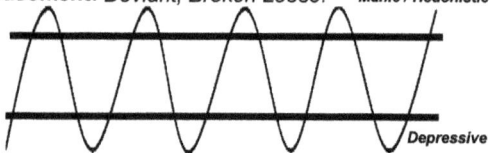

Depressive

The basement is the home of ungovernable needs and desires. It is most often the retreat of the hurting, the broken, and the wounded. Those whose childhood was spent in the attic or the basement of dysfunction, pain, abuse, or trauma may find that the basement is the only comfortable place to live a life molded by pain. The basement contains the soil in which addictions, self-destructive life styles, and irrational thinking can take root and bear fruit. It is the place where demonic influence most easily finds entrance. Human distortions and mental/emotional deformities occur. Oh, how desperately Father seeks those of us, born in a stable and raised in the living room, to mature enough to be sent to those in the attic or commissioned to engage those in the basement!

Both the attic and the basement are escapes from the inability to manage life in the living room. The world is looking for tangible people who know how to live in a real living room. Jesus modeled a living room by living humanly as God intended. He lived there with His father. He taught his disciples how to live there. He sent his disciples out to invite the rest of the world to join them.

God has come in the person of His son to call us down from the attic and up from the basement. Christ teaches us how to function in the reality of the living room as real humans, in a real world, with real people. The Living Room is our stable. Sometimes it smells, is a bit messy, is not as comfortable as we would like, and not everyone behaves with the best manners. But it is where He desires to abide with us. It is the place of His invisible government, the place where we will mature, become fruitful, and learn what is pleasing to Father.

Father imparts Christ into our human experience as an incarnation. Supernatural humanity will be matured in us. The Lord allows us to visit the attic and spend time in the basement so that we know how to help those who are trapped there. When we learn to dwell in the living room, we are able show others genuine compassion and an authentic relationship with the Lord. We are walking with the Lord--human as God created us to be.

How many times have you prayed, "Your Kingdom come, Your will be done, on earth as it is in heaven?" I have prayed that prayer thousands of times, yet I feel I am just now beginning to understand the cosmic implications of these simple words. At the consummation of the age "the kingdom of this world will become the Kingdom of our Lord and of His Christ; and He will reign forever and ever."[25] Notice the kingdom of this world does not disappear; it becomes the Lord's Kingdom. Jesus said, "I make all things new." He did not say, "I make all new things." He makes all things new—including the kingdom of this world.

---

25 Revelation 11:15

This new heaven and earth is born in Christ and in us.

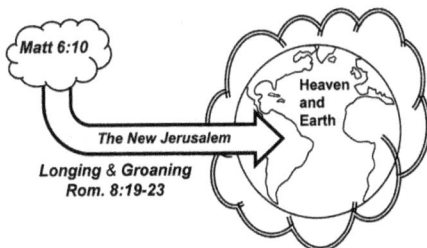

Birthing is a painful experience. Paul tells us:

> For the <u>anxious longing</u> of the creation waits eagerly for the <u>revealing of the sons of God</u>. For the creation was subjected to futility, not willingly, but because of Him who subjected it, in hope that the creation itself also will be set free from its slavery to corruption <u>into the freedom of the glory of the children of God</u>. For we know that the <u>whole creation groans and suffers the pains of childbirth</u> together until now. And not only this, but also we ourselves, having the first fruits of the Spirit, even we ourselves groan within ourselves, waiting eagerly for our adoption as sons, the redemption of our body.[26] [Underlines mine]

---

26 Romans 8:19-23

The "revealing of the sons" identifies the body of Christ coming to functional maturity, fully capable of revealing and imparting the image of the Son. It affirms the Kingdom as invading earth with the governing principles of the New Jerusalem, even as Jesus did. We must recognize and embrace a measure of groaning and longing as our birth pangs. Peter tells us that in the resurrection of Jesus, God "put an end to the agony (Greek, 'birth pangs') of death," which Christ suffered in his passion and death. Birth pangs and real human weakness precede resurrection. He meets us in the stable, and there He begins the work of a New Creation.[27]

The purpose of God endures. We are part of something eternal, immutable, and inevitable. Jesus called this the treasure and the pearl. We must grasp how important it is that we hear His voice. We must recognize we are a stable in which God's ultimate purpose is being born. From the stable we become participants in Father's governing purpose invading earth until the will of God is done here on the earth.

We must commit ourselves to properly respond to God's voice. The creation is anticipating the manifestation of the glory of God. Just before Jesus' ascension He says, "All authority has been given to me in heaven and on earth." Jesus wants to express that authority through us. If He has been given all authority in heaven and earth, the ramifications are that He cannot have more or different authority

27 2 Corinthians 5:17

when He comes. Such reality, seen and embraced, provides the motive and courage for us to prepare ourselves for an extended journey as compared to a hundred-yard dash!

We are the instruments of the *incarnational invasion*. This is the nature of the Kingdom and God's purpose for His Church and for each of us. We are embracing Father God's eternal purpose. We are in the living room! We are seeking how to make ourselves available to participate with Christ in the restoration of God's Fatherhood for the inhabited earth.

We cannot, we must not, view the coming of the Kingdom of God on the earth with the carnal eyes of triumphalism and imperialism. The institutional church has, most often, throughout her history prostituted herself with political and imperial structures. Jesus taught that life comes out from death; ruling from serving; strength from weakness; honor from humility; and wholeness from suffering. If all things are to be made new, it will be through the cross.

Some may ask at this point: What about judgment? Where is the wrath of God, the tribulation, Armageddon, the Lake of Fire? The judgment of God is present in every aspect of His purpose—it is a part of the birth pangs. Our problem has been that we focus more on the particulars of retribution than on the process of redemption. Focus on "end time" particulars tends to become a distraction, keeping us from staying focused on what really matters. Oh, that we could be free from wanting to punish those who do not agree with us.

Embrace Agape as the only workable absolute.

Agape is Love. It is the Father's DNA extended through the death and resurrection of Jesus Christ. It is God's primary governing force. It transforms a corrupt creation to reconcile Heaven and Earth. Agape is the ultimate dynamic of all creation and redemption. C. Baxter Kruger wrote in his wonderful book, *Jesus and the Undoing of Adam:*

> The first thing to be said about the death of Jesus Christ is that he died because God the Father almighty loves us with an implacable and undaunted and everlasting love, a love that absolutely refuses to allow us to perish. [28]

In 1984, I experienced a deep personal crisis. I was on my face wondering if I would physically survive the intensity of my angst. During this time, the Lord said, *"Will you follow Agape wherever it takes you?"*

The only way I could respond was, "Yes." I had the courage to say yes because I had come to

28 Kruger, C. Baxter. *Jesus and the Undoing of Adam.* Perichoresis Press. Kindle Edition.

understand that God is Agape. God as Love is not a doctrine or a principle. It is not one of His attributes (part of God's nature). *It is His essence, His very person and being!* It is the power of God manifested in the physical universe. Agape is manifested in the incarnation. It is the motivation of Jesus' ministry; the very strength of the cross; the source of the resurrection; and the underlying theme of the book of Acts. Agape is manifested today when we pray for others. It releases the power of God for healing and deliverance.

Agape is the essence of everything that has to do with Christ and His Kingdom. Paul writes, "For the whole Law is fulfilled in one word, in the statement, 'You shall love your neighbor as yourself.'"[29] Paul was governed by one word, "The love of Christ controls us."[30] He would declare that you can have all revelation, perform miracles, give away all you have, die as a martyr and end up as nothing if you are not controlled by Agape. Love is what we should pursue.[31] It must be the goal of all instruction and ministry.[32]

An absolute is: "something that is not dependent upon external conditions; something that is free from any restriction or condition; something that is independent of some or all relations; something

---

29 Galatians 5:14

30 2 Corinthians 5:14.

31 1 Corinthians 14:1

32 1 Timothy 1:5

that is perfect or complete."[33] If we examine this definition carefully, we will understand that God is, in Himself, an absolute. Therefore, Agape is an absolute.

He exercises His Love apart from obligation or personal satisfaction. He loves without any desirability or worth in the object of His Love. God is free and seeks to make us free. Agape is His route to freedom.

I have written extensively about Agape[34] so I will not belabor this section further. However, I would leave you with this most expensive challenge: *Are you willing to be governed by one word?* If you are to be governed by a word, you must accept the yoke with Christ in authentic altruism.

In part 2 of *Things That Matter*, I will explore the invitation to be yoked with Christ in authentic altruism. We will consider that God's first and most encompassing statement of blessing was to "all the families of the earth". We will look at the biblical solution of giving a hurting world their Father back. God is the Father of all fathers. The origin of family is rooted in His nature.

---

33 Dictionary.com

34 *Agape Road: A Journey to Intimacy with the Father.*
Available from *lifechangers.org* and Amazon.

LIFECHANGERS®

P.O. Box 3709 ❖ Cookeville, TN 38502
931.520.3730 ❖ lc@lifechangers.org